Murmurings

Murmurings

Poems by

Susan Webber

© 2024 Susan Webber. All rights reserved.
This material may not be reproduced in any form, published,
reprinted, recorded, performed, broadcast,
rewritten, or redistributed without
the explicit permission of Susan Webber.
All such actions are strictly prohibited by law.

Cover design by Shay Culligan
Cover image by Ellie Harold

ISBN: 978-1-63980-620-1

Kelsay Books
502 South 1040 East, A-119
American Fork, Utah 84003
Kelsaybooks.com

For my children Amelia, Brent, and Garrett,
who make me proud to be their mother.

Acknowledgments

Thanks to my dear departed muse, Beeby Pearson. Thank you to my poetry group (Shari, Norman, Kathleen, Georgette, Dana), who keep me disciplined and honest. Thank you to family and friends who provided guidance and kind suggestions (Pam, Tom, and Emily Cavanagh, Peter and David Maine, Polly Harold, Mindy Ross, Joel Solonche). To my son Brent Alberghini, thanks for his love and technical support. To my cousin Ellie Harold, thanks for the lovely cover painting. Lastly, many thanks to Karen and the team at Kelsay Books for appreciating the murmurings of an 80-year-old poet.

Contents

Murmurings	13
Decatur Street	14
Pentimento of Putnam Valley	16
Whip	18
First Kiss	19
Packing the Car for Summer	21
Mother's Day	23
Present	24
He Takes Very Little	25
Naming	26
Moving	28
Houses	29
Sunday Styles	30
Worship	31
Valentine's Day Eve	33
Happy Valentine's Day, Kent	34
Wind	35
This Is What Love Looks Like	36
Forever Friend	37
Quartet	38
Address Book	39
Free Table	41
Morning	42
Danger	43
Column	44
Poetry Group	45
Sun	46
Iris	47
Fall	48
Snow White	49
Leave It	50
Man in the Moon	51
Ma	52

Firstborn	53
My Son, My Sun	54
For Garrett, at 40	55
Saving Grace	59
Blue Butterfly	61
Going	62
Wide-Angle Lens	63
A la Forrest Gump	64
Separation	66
To Julie	67
Reality	68
Revival	69
Ghosts	72
Dancing Meadow Farm	74
Big Beef	75
Who?	77
PTSD	79
Sing	80
Gun Control	81
Benches	82
Stop	83
Road Rage	85
Thich Nhat Hanh	86
Mary Brent	87
Seduction	89
Cat	91
Lesson Learned	92
Rescue	93
The Blues	95
Night in the Pandemic	96
Long COVID	97
The Kiss	98
Paradise Lost	99

As Time Goes By	100
Unburdened	101
Aging in Place	102
The Big D	103
Day and Night	104
Battleground	106
Time Tempering	108
Giving	109
I Remember When . . .	111
Skype	112
Time and Again	113
Settling	114
How Will I Know?	115
The End	116

Murmurings

After she feeds us
My mother
Smooths her hair
Applies lipstick and powder
In front of the old, spotted
Medicine cabinet mirror
In the laundry room.

My father arrives fresh
From the bar car on the
7:05 from New York City
The clink of ice cubes in glasses
And the low murmur of voices
From the living room
Announces the start of evening.

Does she already know about the affair?
In soft, soothing tones, is this where they speak
Of divorce, of suicide?

And we, our bellies full
Our lives secure
In these daily routines
Do not even notice
The change in temperature.

Decatur Street

We visit our grandmother Julie
In the Bed-Stuy brownstone
She shares with her sister and brother-in-law
Aunt Clara and Uncle Clarence

Three stories high
That brown stone almost red
Wide, steep stairs, solid stone sides and railing
Carved double doors, glass-fronted
Though we enter through the basement iron gate
Into the dim underground passage
Glimpsing dining room
Then kitchen at the far end
An open door to the small garden
Sheds light onto the cement floor

On the first floor
We sit with the adults in the back parlor
As they serve drinks from the tray
Ice tinkling in the glasses of whiskey
We sip sparkling ginger ale
As their talk drones on
We slip out to find the marbles in the cigar box
Behind the cushion in the seat under the stairs

Then clamber up to Julie's third floor rooms
To finger buttons in boxes
To gaze out the tall windows
At the city street below
My sister tells me years later
She found a small gun with a mother-of-pearl handle
In the bedside drawer

We enter the tiled bathroom with silver fixtures
And a chain to pull for toilet flushing
How many times did we flush?
The soap in a white ceramic dish I later discover is Dove
Its scent forever set in time
My father's narrow childhood room is at the back
Its single bed still made up
Silent, alone

Dinner in the middle of the afternoon
Is taken in the lower dining room
Small windows at sidewalk height
Light dappling the Chinese evergreens
Cultivated by Uncle Clarence
One of which I still have in my home today
Over a hundred years old
Clarence sits at the head of the table
Ruler of his small dominion
My father and the three women
Bowing to his bluster

We three girls are sent out
To buy a quart of ice cream
At the corner store
The only time we ever see black faces
As we run to and from
To return with melting ice cream
To escape the fear of getting caught

Pentimento of Putnam Valley

Steep steps angle down
To Roaring Brook
Where, on hot summer days,
We splash in the deep, cold waterhole
Scramble up on mossy rocks
Eat peanut butter and jelly sandwiches
On Wonder Bread
Delivered by our mother
Who toils up and down
And swears that all those steps
Enable her to give birth
With just one pain
To our baby brother.

We three sisters walk barefoot
To Tompkin's Corners
Buy Tops Bubble Gum and Mars Bars
All of which we consume
Before we get home.
Pam steps on a yellow jacket nest
And never walks barefoot again.

Red, a high-strung setter
Our first and only dog,
Jumps on us,
Scratching and ripping our clothes.
Confined to a run,
He escapes one day,
Runs in the road and is hit by a car.

In the dim, musty attic of the rural school
We kindergartners gather our blankets
From the low lengths of clothesline
(Mine, soft blue and pink plaid)
And lie for nap time on little cots
Coddled to sleep by stories
Read to us by Mrs. Lamb.

The Bogies, our neighbors
Raise sheep and grill
Homemade German sausages for us
After the dusty shearing is done.
Kay Thompson, on the hill
Across the road,
Offers us cookies and milk
If we can evade her bulldogs
I later learn she authored
The Eloise books.

On Sundays, our father chauffeurs us
To the Mission Church in the village.
Built in the manner of an Iroquois longhouse,
Tall totems at the entrance,
Its cavernous, echoing interior
Smelling of sweet cedar.
He doesn't come in with us
Being non-religious
Nor does my mother
Being agoraphobic
We don't question either absence.

Whip

On Opperman's Pond
We sit on hard, cold rocks
Tug on our white skates
Stiff with newness
Totter onto deep dark ice
Until we get our ice legs
To glide smoothly
In circles, fast forward
Or backward in S formation
When enough of us arrive
We join hands in a line
Those at the front
Pulling the rest
Then quickly changing direction
So we at the end
Accelerate in a wide arc
Screaming and laughing
Breaking apart, only to
Begin again, over and over
Until our feet become numb
Our noses run
And our dads come
To drive us home

First Kiss

I was lucky
It didn't involve
Force or disgust
It might have been with Dave
Junior High
In my old yearbook,
I find a picture of us
In the matching sweaters
I bought us for Christmas
His arm around my shoulder
He was sweet, gentle
It didn't go beyond that
Only young emerging feelings

High School doesn't include him
Many other boys, many other kisses
All wanted, accepted
A long marriage
Full of affection
Ends abruptly
A lover discovered

High school reunion
Feeling sixteen, at fifty
Dave arrives again
Still sweet, tentative
And he responds, quietly
With many thanks
We spend Easter in Hawaii
He from one side of the globe
I from another

Then he is gone
Into distance and death
His gentle nature
And kisses remain

Packing the Car for Summer

High-backed beach chairs from Costco
New, colorful striped towels
That will dry quickly

Coffee cups and wine glasses
Blue and white dish towels
Pots of basil and oregano and white bacopa

Two cases of Pinot Grigio
Purchased at 18% discount on a Tuesday
At the wine store in New Paltz

Piles of shorts and faded cotton shirts
A new black and turquoise bathing suit
Which will go well with the turquoise beach hat
Stuffed in the old camp duffel
That still smells of last year's mildew

A box containing books and
Knitting projects from winter
Still uncompleted
And bags of medicine vials and creams
Everyday ones, and ones for "What if,
God forbid?"

Sparklers, Bat-Man Puzzles, an orange plastic
Horse Shoe Game
Which will be fought over and strewn
And used as weapons for which they
Were not designed

The old, silver computer and DVDs
And new, large cushioned ear phones
To block out loud, wine-fueled voices
From the porch

Finally, beloved 18-year-old Moustache
In his carrier on the front seat
Already heavy lidded and limp
From the tranquilizer pills

Car packed with hope and dread

Mother's Day

On my visit home,
I pick her a posy
Of purple violets
Their green heart-shaped leaves
Hugging the tiny blossoms

The next week, inside too long,
She exclaims over the bright flowers
In the garden
As they wheel her
Into the ambulance

On Mother's Day, at the Catholic hospice
I offer my three young children
Knowing she cherishes
Their clear faces and grubby hands
Filling them with candy and kisses

But she ignores them and me
Absorbed in the TV coverage
Of the shooting of the Pope
She, like he, halfway
To the promised land

He survives, she steps over
But every spring
Around Mother's Day
She rises from the moist, fertile earth
In her purple and green finery

Present

I hear the stirring upstairs
And slip into the early dawn
The Christmas tree and presents
Arrayed in the quiet, empty room

The two brothers
Ten and six
Creep down the stairs
In their reindeer pajamas
Bumping each other
Murmuring excitedly
Their eyes devouring the presents
Believing in the mystery

And I, kissing their warm, sleep-infused heads
Whisper "Merry Christmas"
Having been given the exquisite gift
Of witnessing their joy

He Takes Very Little

He takes very little
Only the table in the basement
Which holds the laundry supplies
And which she, out of long habit,
Helps him dust off
And carry to his car,
Putting the detergent and
Drier sheets on the floor.

And the pull-out couch
With the mattress-ticking cover
Residing in the light-filled dining room
Which they open up and sleep on
When his parents come to visit
And where they recently sat
To discuss the dissolution of their marriage

After he has gone
She cleans the gaping space it has left
Every time she enters the room
Its absence a stabbing pain
She quickly replaces it
Yet the old one retains its ghostly presence
Amid the blue flowered upholstery

Naming

I change my name
After my divorce
I do not go back
To my maiden name
Who wants to slide back
Into a state of maidenhood,
Of innocent youth?
Someone whom I am not now
Nor ever will be again.

I take my mother's
Birth name of Webber
Webber, weaver of webs
Connected to maternal roots
Weaver of new life
Woven to a fresh fabric
It feels fresh
And right
My name is Webber.

I do the paperwork myself
Filling in the forms
With my new name
Again and again
Filing them
With the government clerk
Becoming more and more familiar
With my new self
My name is Webber.

I tell my friends and family
Of my name change
But they often forget
And introduce me to others
As my former self
It irritates me
I am no longer that person
I am another
My name is Webber.

Finally, I compose a song
To sing to them
When they get me wrong:

"My name is Sue Webber
I'll have it forever
It's the name I've chosen to be
When I walk down the street
All the people I meet
They say, "What is your name?"
And I say,
"My name is Sue Webber
I'll have it forever . . ."

Moving

Moving out of an old house
Is like shedding a skin
The hard part is getting a finger hold
At the top of my head
And working it slowly and carefully
So that it comes off in one piece

Some days, it won't budge at all
On others, I notice a whole piece
Has peeled away with no effort on my part
And then there are the bits that stick and pull
The pain is stabbing or just plain irritating
The place around the heart is the most difficult

Sometimes I wonder if it is worth it
Growing a new skin and shedding the old
But, like a child finally giving up her beloved,
ratty old blanket
It is inevitable, and, once begun,
there is no turning back
As more old skin is unmoored,
it becomes an albatross
That must be dragged around, tripped over,
and sometimes carried

When moving day comes
And the old house is stripped bare
I close the door for the last time
Shake my foot a little to release
the last bit of old skin
And leave it dry, brittle, piled up on the doorstep
With one final glance backward
I can see it sigh and settle into itself

Houses

When I move from one house to another
It is to create a new life
The new house is red, and bright
With many windows
It speaks welcome

The old place has burned down
A cremation of years
The new has lived and thrived
These past ten years
The little red house
On a country road

Sunday Styles

I still read Sunday Styles
In the New York Times
Even though, for years,
I have searched the faces
Of happy couples
For the 50% who will divorce
Sooner or later
Hatred, infidelity, indifference
Replacing "till death do us part"

Weddings are my least favorite ritual
Over-the-top clothing and food
Professional photography
Erasing any flaws in the perfect picture
Joy and hope going forward
"A day you will never forget"
Though, maybe in a way
Not expected,
Were the seeds of failure
Growing that very day?

My own son is divorcing
One out of two married children
Which would be 50 percent
Satisfying the research results

His ex-wife, one of two children
Will now satisfy the statistic

My brother and I
Of four siblings
Meet the criteria

Yet I still read the Sunday Styles
In the New York Times

Worship

We gather in the basement
Of the church
Sitting on folding chairs
Twenty or so souls
In need of refreshment
Of solace

Some of us know one another
Some are strangers
A flock facing our spirit guide
In need of unity
Of community

She hands out the liturgy
Familiar to many
Begins her magic
Using only a portable keyboard
And voice

We proceed in halting fashion
Going over the words
Starting again and again
Refining our understanding
In unison and harmony

After two hours
We become a congregation
Strangers no more
Singing an offering to the afflicted world
In one joyful chorus

"I see your true colors shining through
I see your true colors
And that's why I love you
So don't be afraid to let them show
Your true colors
True colors are beautiful
Like a rainbow"

Amen

Valentine's Day Eve

They have been separated for six months
He is living on his own now
His wife and two boys
In the family home

He asks his older son, age 12
Whether he bought a gift, made a card
For his mother
The answer is, "No."

On the way to drop off his son
They stop at the store
Buy the big red heart chocolates
And bouquet of flowers

Pull in the driveway in the dark
The car lights illuminate the open garage
They hide the heart and flowers
Under the workbench

He reminds his son
To make a personal card
Then gathers him into a hug
The car lights silhouetting their
Two forms into one

Happy Valentine's Day, Kent

I pick up the small, beige book at the library
Our Souls At Night, by Kent Haruf
I turn to the picture of the author on the back cover.
Older man, white hair receding,
trim mustache, blue denim shirt, glasses.
A shadow of a smile which extends to his eyes,
connecting with mine.
Now that's someone I would like to get to know.

The book is deep and slow
Like I knew it would be
from his photograph.
I am smitten.

I turn to the blurb on the inside.
A listing of previous novels, awards.
And then, "He died in November 2014, at the age
of seventy-one."
I was seventy-one in November, 2014.
Now, three years later, never having known him,
I grieve his loss.
Happy Valentine's Day, Kent.

Wind

I have holes in my brain
Wind whistles softly in the spaces

My husband and grown girls
Still have names and I know I love them
But they seem to lean away from me

The house looks the same
Yellow walls, bamboo couch, vintage rugs
But my connection to it is tenuous

The car, the one plastered
with so many years of stickers,
Which I drove alone and free
Scares me

The phone, too
Because I don't know these people who call
And can't quite write the messages they leave

The garden, my passion,
Has faded from lack of water
or drowned from too much
The hours I spent there have turned to minutes

Time has lost its meaning
You were gone so long
Even though you insist it was just an hour

My brain is abuzz with effort
Trying to bridge the empty spaces
The soft whistling turns to a howling wind
I need to rest now, to sleep
Please, just let me sleep

This Is What Love Looks Like

Not the early fluttering
Of flirting recognition
Not the first dinners
Movies, walks in the forest
Not the hands touching
Kisses tentative and electric
Or even the nights of intimacy
Not the pledges of exclusivity
Or the easy familiarity of routine

Love is the sharing of bad news
Of talking and talking
Of encouragement, of loneliness, of fear
Love is the hours of practical labor
Of doctor visits, insurance claims, bus schedules
Of exhaustion
Of getting up again the next day
Not knowing the future
But being there
Month after month, day after day, hour after hour
This is what love looks like

Forever Friend

I go to the market
To prepare for yet another winter storm
I buy the clamshell strawberries
Too expensive
The ripe few in view
Hiding the rest with the pale green tops
I picture the pickers
Stoop laboring, plucking the unripe fruit
From unwilling stems
I plan to slice them atop my morning oatmeal
Some semblance of color
In these cold, white days

But, you, forever friend,
Have bent forward in the July heat
Sweat sliding down your back
Picking fully vine-ripened gems
Rinsing, hulling, chopping
Adding just a bit of sugar
To their already sweet nectar
Stirring over the hot stove
On a hot day
Filling the little mason jars
Topped with red and green calico
For my Christmas gift

Forever friend
You have saved
Summer in a jar
For me to spread on my toast
This frigid winter morning

Quartet

The wee house rests quietly
Facing the mist-covered mountains
In the distance.

As if painted on the inside window
A white cat sits, tall and statue still
Watching, as, outside the fence,

Two dogs, one large and black
The other, small and brown
Bark companionably in harmony.

In front, a delicate, black and russet feline
Grooms herself in the grass.

Quartet of guardians to the soul within

Address Book

My address book
is at least twenty years old
I finally find a replacement
Not so easy
in this era of cell phones,
numbers and e-mails
stored in a small device

The old book is tattered,
with notes and folded
papers sticking out of it
So many names are people
I have not seen or heard from
in years,
numbers and addresses obsolete

Some are dead
I remember who they were
as I delete their names
Whole stories from the past
rise up from the book,
float through my mind

Some are old colleagues
whom I had occasionally
tried to call
and whose numbers come up empty
Others are neighbors and friends
from old lives,
all of us having moved on

The section on doctors
is confused by crossouts,
changes and deletions,
numbers up the sides of the pages
I enter mostly new doctors,
additions of specialties not needed
when I was young

It takes a few sessions
to complete the changeover,
get rid of the stray papers
and become the owner of a tidy,
up-to-date book
I throw out the old tattered one
My past in the trash

Free Table

I raise the shades
And gaze out the window
Onto the country road
As I do my morning exercises

A runner with a dog on a leash
Pauses to peruse
The "free table" at the edge
Of my neighbor's driveway

Yesterday, I placed there
An old Christmas tree stand
A dusty Britta water filter
Two large ironstone platters

Little language dictionaries
In French, Italian, Spanish
A tall wooden CD holder
Painted with red and yellow flowers

I watch as the runner considers
Picking up one item and another
Decides on the heavy CD holder
And lumbers home

I smile broadly
Her load is her treasure
My load lightens

Morning

I sit at the table
Sipping fragrant coffee
Yellow placemat
Checkered cloth napkin

Outside, snow lightens
The winter landscape
Rain comes softly
Darkening bare branches

As I read the morning news
Of atrocities in Syria
Outside
The trees weep

Danger

The morning after first frost
Canvas-covers draped over
The tender lettuce
By the migrant workers
Look like tents for refugees
Who come here to plant,
Tend and harvest the lettuce
For us to consume without thinking.

Huddled in rows
Safe for the moment
From killing cold.
In late afternoon,
Their protection is thrown off
And the lettuce is free
To drink in the sun and grow.
Unlike the refugees,
Where danger lies in every field
On every street.

Column

February thaw
The ice-clogged river
Mostly melted
Except for about a foot
At the edges

On which stand
Canadian geese.
Not sitting,
Crowded in communion,
But standing in a line
Silent, erect
Facing south
One after the other
So many, maybe one hundred

While we stand
Wait in ticket lines
In grocery lines
In coffee lines
Jostling, grousing
Moving from one foot to the other
Talking on cell phones, texting

The geese stand erect,
Silent
Facing south
In the February thaw

Poetry Group

It is again the day before
Our poetry meeting
And the page is blank
Christmas has come and gone
Although I did finally manage
To get my tree lit on the porch
It still shines out into the cold
On these long winter nights

The New Yorker jigsaw puzzle
From my daughter
The one with a thousand brown bikes
Remains mostly undone on the counter
One more week of frustration
And I will donate it to the library

My visit to Plymouth
For Jon's 80th birthday party
Is cut short by impending snow
But I spend sweet hours in the car
With my son Garrett
So rare to speak alone together

I visit Jessie in the hospital
She has struggled so much in the
Last months and years
It seems hospice is the next step
Yet her eyes are clear
And sense of humor intact

The sun is bright today
Tomorrow is my poetry group

Sun

Filters through gauzy curtains
As I wake in the morning

Shines on bare legs
As I rise from my bed

Warms my back
As I sip my coffee

Suffuses the room
As I raise roman shades

Spotlights yellow wheat
On the side of the road

Spins through filmy tail
Of zigzagging squirrel

Highlights south windows
Of the stately brick house

Reddens the barn side
Leaves the rest in shadow

Flares five orange tulips
In the dining room vase

Coddles me in comfort
As I lie on the couch

Iris

Amid the cold autumn wind
And the dead brown stalks
Stands a white iris
Trembling

An abandoned bride
Her veil rippling
Stands shocked and confused
At the empty altar

Fall

The orange leaves frantically
Wave to me.
A few, then a hundred
Unhitch themselves
And fly toward me
Kissing my hair, my cheek,
My neck
Then fall to the path
To be crushed by me, their lover

More fly, thousands.
More kisses,
More death.

Snow White

As I walk
I see bits of white
On the edges
Of the road
And in the field
And wonder
Why they survived
The melting snow

It is not snow
But tufts of snow-white feathers
Still fresh and fluffy
Scattered along the roadway
Where the chickens once clucked

I used to cluck with them
In companionable friendship
But now my mind hears
Their wild screeching
Sees the flapping of wings
As they shed their feathers in terror

Leave It

Fall happens late
Weather warm and wet
Turning leaves brown
A disappointment of color

But the Japanese maples
Make an unexpected splash
A late-season hit
Garbed in red-orange-pink

The one in my yard
Announces its beauty
For a few short days
A star amid drab company

Then rains pound
At last the sun appears
Illuminating empty branches
Yet on the ground
A circle of red-orange-pink
Leaves all on the stage

Man in the Moon

The night is inky
The full moon emerges
From fast-moving clouds
Bright white
But so sad
His face looking at me
Through the kitchen window
Grey wrinkles
Pulling down his features
Eyes half closed
Cheeks sunken
Mouth turned down

Gazing at the earth from afar
He asks in perplexed silence,
"How could you despoil your garden?
How could you contaminate your home?
How could you hate, torture, and kill
Other species and your own?
How could you mock the beauty of life?"

The moon moves behind the clouds
Hiding from what he sees

Ma

The phone rings at 8 am
I look at the number
No Caller ID
But for some reason
I answer it

First there is that silence
Of a robo-call
Or fund-raising effort
I don't know why I hang on
But I do

I say, "Hello"
And then a louder
More irritated, "Hello"
A young, male on the other end
Says, "Hi, Ma"

It is neither of my two sons
Now grown beyond this boy's tone
"Who is this?" I demand.
With a catch in his voice,
He says, "Ma, it's Anthony"

But I am not Anthony's Ma
"No honey," I say quietly
"I am not your Ma."
"You have the wrong number"

He is so sorry
We hang up
I think of him often
Needing his Ma
Wanting her voice

Firstborn

Firstborn
Birthed on Martha's Vineyard
One month late
After long, hard labor

A daughter, Amelia
Whose reluctance to be born
Speaks of strong ties
To her mother

Beautiful, curly-haired blond
Soulful brown eyes
Independent spirit from the start
Such grace and confidence
Admired by all

Two younger brothers
A loving father
Summers on the Vineyard
At the Crystal Palace

Amelia
46 years old today
Husband, children, dog
House on her native Vineyard

Generous spirit
Ties to her mother
Still strong
Such love
Such grace

My Son, My Sun

Forty-one years ago today
St. Francis Hospital
Port Jervis, New York
As the sun is rising
A son is born

Liquid brown eyes
Mop of curly blond hair
Dark skin like his grandfather
A smile that charms all
My son, my sun

A man now
Strong muscular body
Tireless worker in all tasks
Sensitive, empathic
My son, my sun

Forty-one years old today
Close acquaintance to heartache
Survivor of hurricanes and earthquakes
Still on course
My son, my sun, my son

For Garrett, at 40

You are two weeks late
Like your brother
Cherishing the safety and warmth
Of the womb just a little longer

When you decide it is time
The two birthing rooms at St. Frances
In Port Jervis, are full
So you are born in the hall
Of the maternity wing
Neither you nor I
Caring where, only that
You are finally making an appearance

Your bilirubin is high
So you are placed in an isolette
In the nursery
Under the lights
Wearing only miniature sunglasses
And a tiny diaper
On your upraised butt

I am devastated that I cannot
Have you in my room with me
But the Chinese doctor keeps smiling
And saying, "Mother knows best!"
While refusing to let you come with me
Finally, the nurses and I hatch a plot
Whereby I sit with you in a rocking chair
Under the lights in the nursery

We are in the hospital for a week
You and I given a precious seven days to admire
Each other and rest in quiet without interruption
A gift of time before the family tumult to come
When we come home
Your older sister, at six, instantly becomes a mother
Your brother, at three, tweaks your nose
And says, "Hi there, Guy Smiley!"

You are a chubby, blond baby
Slow to cry
Able to hold your own
Among the many children and caregivers
In your young life
You walk at 10 months, and climb, too
So I follow you around until your brain
Catches up with your sturdy little legs

That first day of summer at the Vineyard
You, at age 15 months
Walk straight into the ocean
Over your head
Until your second mother yells
And I run and scoop you out

Your early walking
Precedes all your athletic prowess
From riding a two-wheeler at four
Doing "pop-a-wheelies," *Look, Mom!*
Playing soccer, baseball, basketball
Both in high school and at the Vineyard
To your consternation, whenever you make a basket
I yell, "That's my boy!"

You remain a stoic
Rarely crying and slow to reveal your feelings
The best place for us is in the car
Where I can voice
What I think you must be feeling
"That must make you angry"
Or where I could ask you a question
Both of us staring straight ahead

You have an honesty
I can only admire
Putting into a few short words
What you must have been thinking
About but not verbalizing
We had our disagreements
But I can always count on you
To be straight with me

I'll never forget seeing you
Coming down the hospital hall
With the nurse and your firstborn son, Adrian
A grin on your face
That I hadn't seen in the previous difficult years
And then Filip is born
Two sons who made you into a man
Giving your life focus and deep commitment

You are at my side
During my various physical challenges
My knee replacement
My health crisis on the Vineyard
Always there, always ready to go

The extra mile
And I know you will remain that strong, steady son

At age 40
You have endured your share of heartache
The early death of your dad
The impending divorce
Yet you retain your wry sense of humor
Your fierce work ethic
Your unwavering commitment to family
"THAT'S MY BOY!"

Saving Grace

You saved another life today
Not counting the hundred families
You feed every week
In your Mexico City food program
Not counting the homeless people
Who know your cellphone number
And to whom you deliver food
Outside the nearby church

Christian runs from home
Lands in the Zona Rosa
Sleeping in the oversized tire
Near the basketball court
Where you go to shoot around

Only fourteen, he is an innocent
Escaping from anger and abuse at home
You give him a winter coat,
Pants, socks, and food
Call sympathetic and safe
Agencies to care for him

Mostly, you listen to him
Believe his pain and confusion
Knowing you could not offer him a home
Much as you yearn to
Soon, with the cellphone you give him
He reaches his mom
Who drives seven hours to Mexico City
To pick him up

She calls to thank you
For your kindness
And ask how she can ever repay you
You say,
You can repay me by taking care of him
And loving him and accepting him
For who he is, no matter what.

You couldn't save Gehenna
You couldn't save Ivan
But today, because of your open heart
You save another life

Blue Butterfly

At the early snowfall
I extend my tongue
To catch a few fat, icy crystals
But, instead, a late blue butterfly
Lands there.

I try to see it
By looking cross-eyed down my nose
If only I had a mirror
Or a friend to exclaim at this miracle.

My jaw grows tight
With the effort of keeping my mouth open
And when the little creature lifts off
With a barely perceptible push
I am just able to whisper
"Farewell, dear friend."

Going

The last snow comes and goes
in the night
Outside my window, I see only the soft, yellow
lights of the plow
Pushing back and forth
on the dark road

In the morning, a chiaroscuro
of bright white and dark shadows paints the ground
Sun warms the blue sky
The road dries to a black path

I walk, shedding my hat and gloves,
loosening my scarf
Hearing birds singing their predictions
of seasons to come

Wide-Angle Lens

Eight deep pink roses
In a blue glass vase
On a green placemat
On an oak table
In the sunny dining room
In the spacious first floor
Of the Craftsman style house
With the red siding
On the one-acre lot
With the maple tree in front
And evergreens in back
On a rural country road
In a small college town
In the state of New York

A la Forrest Gump

I was there
in Washington D.C.
when JFK died in Dallas,
and stood for eight hours
with the grieving crowd
to watch the cortège
pass by,
stirrups on the
empty horse
facing backward.

I was there
in London, England
when Churchill died,
and followed thousands
headed to Westminster Abbey
for the elaborate funeral
None of us admitted,
but only needing
to be near
the historic event.

I was there
on Martha's Vineyard
when Mary Jo Kopechne died
in the waters off Dike Bridge,
and Edward Kennedy
swam the Chappaquiddick channel
in the dark summer night
to call his family
and his lawyer.

I was there
on Martha's Vineyard
when JFK Jr. died
in the single engine plane
that went down in the fog,
taking with him
his fiancé and her twin sister,
and plunging his family
and the country
into grief yet again.

Here in my life
I am witness
to the unfamous deaths
of dear family and friends,
and will continue
until I witness my own.

Separation

How ironic
As I struggle
To lose weight
Denying myself
Pasta, chocolate, wine
You cannot find the appetite
To keep yourself strong
No morsels of tempting food
Arouse your desire

How ironic
As I am able
To go off the prednisone
And can wear my watch and ring
The inflammation fading
You are increasing
The chemo drugs
Cancer growing
Inside your body

How ironic
As I crave more time with you
To share the full white moon
Fall leaves in bright clothing
To laugh and cry together
You are slipping away
Into the contemplation of death
Separating to do the solitary work
Of transition

The moon is waning
Leaves are falling
The sky clouds over
Rain is predicted

To Julie

Your photograph
Of the dandelion
Sun-shot through white
Seeds about to fly off
With the slightest breeze
Each delicate spore
Settling in a separate space
Of the wind's choosing

Your mother died
Seven years ago
Her body at the end
Lighter than air
Ready to fly off free
Her spore landing
Growing, all the world over
Seeding art
Love taking root

Reality

Sitting at the dining table
Reading about possible Netflix movies
I glance out the window
See the impossibly red cardinal
Perched on the grey-brown branches
Of the nearby crabapple tree
Snow a background of white

He is looking at me
Between the pink Christmas ornament
And red stained-glass apple
I have hung in the window
To prevent the birds from the feeders
From smashing into the glass

Revival

In the early morning,
I enter the Campgrounds.
Quiet reigns.

Cottages perch cheek to cheek
Pastel colored confections
Freshly painted
Built in 1867, 1868, 1869
Names on hand-lettered signs:
Crystal Palace, La Vie en Rose
Absolut Heaven, Goff to the Beach

Every house has a porch
Snuggled shoulder to shoulder
So close that one could hold hands
With a neighbor next door.
Hanging baskets of petunias, begonias
Ivy geraniums sway in the breeze

Gardens abound with hydrangeas
Of every hue
Zinnias, cornflowers, impatience
Crowd together in the wee spaces
Velvet indigo morning glories climb
Up porch posts
Orange trumpet vines drape their
Finery around eaves

Screen doors start to open
An artist sits on her porch
with her easel
Paints the front of the cottage
Across the lane
A little boy bumps his scooter
Down the porch steps
Chubby legs appear in a carriage
Baby face invisible under the hood

Birds skitter, twitter
Telephone wires tremble
As squirrels tightrope
Tabby curls on a rocking chair cushion
A small girl in an orange sundress
Walks her stuffed bunny in a stroller
Squats down to sniff purple flowers
A young boy with bare feet tucked
Under him, reads a book

The smell of bacon frying
Clinking of forks on plates
Families, even children, sit silently
On small porches, spooning cereal
Before a long day at the beach

Neighbors make their quiet way
Onto porches, down steps,
Across the lanes
To murmur to each other
Discuss families arriving, departing
Commiserate over absences,
Illness, death

A wooden bench provides a resting spot
Its copper plaque reads,
In loving memory of Bill and Bonnie Brown
How many have come to this revival?
How many still do?
Only the porches know.

Ghosts

There are ghosts on these streets
Their faces appear on the porches
We have walked by for so many summers
Greeting them on the way to the beach with,
"How was your winter?"

Our next-door neighbors Kay and Joe
And Mary and Bill Thomas
Mary is on the roof sweeping away the leaves
Barney and Despina in their little house
With the two apartments
Mary, of the Summer Place, on her way
To Reliable Market for fresh rolls
Ed and Madeline Rhodes
Regal in bearing, soft in speech
The three Thomas sisters,
Pressing coins into the palms
Of our newborn babies
Reggie Tucker and his wife
Who owned the Tucker Inn
Lawrence of the booming voice and dreadlocks
Bea and Bill, Gloria, and Lou
Sylvia Roses with her silver-haired bun
And her husband Joe, the dentist
"Hello, hello"

And our own beloved
All gone, all ghosts,

Appearing as we round the corners
Eleanore and Fred
Margaret and Albert
Kay, Joe, and Jack
Aunts Charlotte and her twin Chris
Peter and Beeby

All gone,
But lingering on the porch rockers
In the summer breeze

Dancing Meadow Farm

No one is dancing
At Dancing Meadow Farm
Winter grief has taken hold
Brittle stalks of grass
Scrape together in the wind
Hard ground unyielding
The sky dark with clouds
No one is dancing
At Dancing Meadow Farm

Yet, some Spring
Maybe not this one
But some Spring
The grasses will turn green
And sway in the breeze
The ground will soften
Making way for new seeds
The sky will brighten
Sun will warm the air

And she at
Dancing Meadow Farm
Will run through the fields
Pick wildflowers
Turn somersaults
On the lush grass
And dance

Big Beef

MMM AWW
You know, guys
This is just heaven
Standing together in this green field
Munching on sweet dew-damp grass
In the warm morning sunlight

Hey, my friends
Just stop for a moment
And look up at the
Rocky Shawangunk Mountains
Dotted with red-orange-yellow colors of fall
I mean, is this not just the best?
MMM AWW

Oh look, fellas
There's our Farmer Bill
On his tractor over near the river
Can you see what's in
The flat-bed he's pulling?
Oh, my God, it's corn fodder
Mixed with hay and sorrel
My favorite!!
MMM AWW

Hey, watch out, buddy
I was first
We'll all get there
But be a little careful
Of who you push out of the way
And those little ones
They'll just have to wait
Until we've had our bellyful

Like I said, compadres
Isn't this just
Our little piece of paradise?
MMM AWW

Who?

Who will rise
In the dim early morning light
Pull on heavy overalls and socks
And stand by the window
Overlooking the rolling meadow
Sipping steaming black coffee

Who will button
The rough canvas jacket
And walk down the dirt road in the cold
As the sun comes up behind him
And enter the dim breathy barn
With the jostling beef cattle

Who will greet
His animals with soft words
Pats, and caresses
And then throw open the barn door
To allow them to crowd out
Down the hill to the edge of the water

Who will watch
As they dip their hooves
Into the cool Wallkill River
And cross slowly to the steep hill
Overlooking the Shawangunk Mountains
SkyTop in the distance

Who will forklift
The round hay bales
To the front of the tractor
Drive it to the meadow
And spread it on the ground
Sniffing its fresh acrid scent

Who will revel
In the turn of the seasons
The natural beauty
The endless days

Jim Dodd is dead.

PTSD

I see Brett Kavanagh again
On the news
Grinning with his new posse
On the Supreme Court
My stomach turns again
As it will whenever I see his face

Brett Kavanagh, ungrown
Entitled frat brat
Angry, immature drinker
Acting to impress his boy gang
Denying what happened so long ago
Because to him it was no big deal

Christine is all girls, all women
Soft, high voice
Ingratiating, uncertain
Smiling on the verge of tears
Her suppressed anger
Disguised as fear

The fury of Brett Kavanagh
And the Republican men
The spitting rage at women
At their Me Too power
To suggest that they, too, have a voice
Even under the smothering hand

When I see Brett Kavanagh
Grinning, confident
I wonder about Christine
How are you doing, dear sister?
I hope you didn't see him
Are you weeping?

Sing

Years ago, we almost moved
To Otisville, NY
The site of the federal prison
Where Michael Cohen now resides

When I sit down to eat a meal
I wonder what he is being served
In the prison mess
Is he able to get special food?

I shouldn't feel sorry for him
Bully fixer for the ultimate bully
Yet I see him as the adolescent acolyte
Desperate for the approval of his boss

The boss who has no trouble
Kicking him to the curb
Michael finally realizing that loyalty
Only goes one way

So sing, Michael, sing
Reveal all you know
About the underbelly of your former world
Sing for your supper

Gun Control

In the dead of dark night
The intruder bursts through the front door
Pounding up the stairs into my bedroom

A loaded gun was not in my bedside drawer
I was not afraid to live alone
When would I need to use one?

But that night I would have used one
As my heart thumped in the dark
I would have used it

Killing my son
Who had raced home from college
When his friend had used one
To try to kill himself

Benches

To catch my breath,
I sit quietly
On the roomy bench
On the bridge
Over the Wallkill River
And look out to the
Shawangunk Mountains
My cane angled beside me

A plaque of dedication
Reads, "Rachel Pekarsky (1964–2014)"
She, I have been told
Was a fierce force for
The rail trail on which she now
Invites me to rest with her

They're removing wooden benches
In Central Park
Replacing them with
Cold, uncomfortable steel
To hamper the homeless
From using them as respite
From the damp ground

Even the metal benches
Now have seat separators
With armrests to prevent
Slouching, leaning, touching
Let not the weak, infirm rest here

Stop

ONE
Flashing lights behind
Cause me to pull over
I expect the police car
To pass me on the way
To an emergency
But it stops behind me
Lights still flashing
I ask myself
If I had been speeding
But, no, I was just on my way
To the gym, in no real hurry

I roll down my window
As the cop approaches
He informs me that both my
Rear brake lights are out
He asks for my license and registration
I lean over to get my purse
Amid my gym bags,
And fumble for the registration
In the glove compartment

TWO
Flashing lights behind
Cause me to pull over
I expect the police car
To pass me on the way
To an emergency

But it stops behind me
Lights still flashing
I ask myself
If I had been speeding
But no, I was just on my way
To the gym, in no real hurry

Heart thudding
I roll down my window
The cop approaches
Asks for my license and registration
As I lean over to get my purse
Amid my gym bags,
He growls, "STOP!"
And orders me out of the car
I sit rigid and ask what the problem is
He says, "Lady, get out of the car
I'll get your IDs"
"Don't touch my stuff," I rage.
"I refuse to get out
Until you tell me
Why you pulled me over."
"You really want to go down that road?" he hisses.
"I'm calling for backup. DON'T MOVE"!

Road Rage

I consider myself
A laid-back, unflappable
Accepting human being
But just yesterday
As I wait at the light in my car
I suddenly realize how wrong I've been

Because I hear myself shouting,
"Go, go, go, you idiot
Can't you see the light is green
And we have mere seconds
Before it turns red again?"

And mere seconds later
Someone in my car is ranting,
"Don't you know how to use your blinker
You blinkin' know nothing!"

I take a few deep breaths
Until I hear the curse at the oblivious jaywalker
Who never looks up from his phone
As he saunters across the street.

As the car tailgating me in traffic
Suddenly passes on the right
And swerves in front of me
I observe someone yell
"Are you happy, you ignoramus
You are now one whole car ahead!"

I pull into my garage
Get out of the car
And once more, assume the mantle
of forgiveness and love.

Thich Nhat Hanh

(1926–2022)

Thay: teacher.
On his photograph,
He writes,
I am free
I am home

Do not grieve me
I am with you
In the new green leaves
In the daisies in the field
In the chickadees at the feeder

I zest the lemon—Thay
I sift flour and sugar—Thay
I stir in eggs, butter, ripe bananas—Thay
I bake and breathe in the aroma—Thay
I savor a warm banana muffin—Thay

Mary Brent

(1923–2023)

When we call
And ask how she is doing
She always says, "Goooood"
Even when she has cancer
Needs a wheelchair
Even when her wedding ring
Is stolen from her room
In the assisted living facility

When we zoom
In small groups
For her hundredth birthday
She beams and remembers
All our names
And our children's names
Sending cards for our birthdays
Addressed in her own hand

When her beloved daughters
First Mary, then Ann, die
She grieves with Harry
But never lets her sadness
Affect her closeness
With the rest of her family
She delights in visits
From Owen and Lucy
To her last days

When Harry dies
She loses half her heart
But realizes she has more work to do
To shore up the ailing,

Emotionally and physically,
And to contribute generously
To family, friends
Caregivers, causes

Her Catholic faith fortifies her
Uplifts her
She never judges
Only listens and supports
Those who don't understand
How a belief in God
Can be a bulwark
Against life's battering

Now she is free
To leave her wheelchair
To leave her devoted Stephen and Pat
To join her sisters Claire, Chrissie,
Charlotte, Eleanore
Brothers Brent and Brud
Her Mary, her Ann
Her Harry

To pray for us
From afar
So that our lives
May be "Gooood."

Seduction

Sometimes
In the too quiet night
And especially when
Snow is falling outside
I am lonely

That is why I adopt another cat

We have a pas de deux, Max and me
He hides in the basement for days
And I visit him to
Search out his frightened eyes
And tempt him with treats and
sweet words.
"Come out, Maxie," I murmur.

He finally relents and
Lets me carry his heavy, reluctant
Body upstairs
As I kick the basement door closed
He retreats again
This time under my bed
"You little devil," I gently scold.

And, when, after more courtship
He emerges
Still shy and suspicious
We circle each other
I initiating more contact
He, aloof yet interested

He has his own bed
Which he loves
And then moves to the chair
Opposite me as I lie on the couch
Soon he relaxes at my feet
"Oh, Max, you are my darling," I gush

Then, he begins to follow me
To every room as I move about
Sitting near me as I cook
Eat my dinner, even as I
Use the toilet

He is waiting at the door
When I arrive home
And brushes against my legs
As I walk

In the morning, he wakes
From his sleep next to my pillow
And scratches the rug
Until I rise to feed him

His eyes adoring
As he moves in front of me
On the stairs
And surprised when I
Step on his tail
And raise my voice at his
Suffocating closeness
"Max, get away," I hiss.

Cat

I am the cat.
Wise in the ways of the world
I hunch in coiled readiness
To kill what I choose
And present it to you
Dead bunnies, mice
Birds shorn of their feathers
Under the bed, in the shower,
Displayed in full view on the floor
I am proud.

I am the cat.
Abundant in fur
Thick in body
I demand food
By jumping in front of you
Or between your feet
Sated, I lounge near you
Or roll over on the floor
And expose my belly
I am unafraid.

I am the cat. Your domesticated tiger
Your lion in waiting
Between two worlds.

Lesson Learned

Glossy, black Tom

Splays on the sunny floor

In front of the French doors,

Their checkered mullions

Casting shadows around him.

On his back, belly exposed,

Front legs stretched out

Over his thrown-back head,

Tail thumping softly

In exaltation

Rescue

Max the Cat is suddenly gone
My 18-pound rescue
Who cannot stop eating
Because he is afraid
He will be hungry again
My big-pawed, tawny-bellied friend
Who greets me at the door
And follows me everywhere
Is suddenly gone

Not into the cold, snowy night
Which he avoids
Having been outside alone for too long
But into the vet's office
The x-ray machine
And the diagnosis
Of fluid on the lungs
The only cure being
A quick, painless death

They bring him to me
In the car
I weep and say goodbye
His eyes on me
Trusting I will do
What is best for him

At home, I wipe out his carrier
And bring it to the basement
I clean his litter

And scoop the poop
I wash his bedding
Vacuum out gray hair
From rugs and furniture

All the while,
Glimpsing him sliding
Around the corners near me
His tail disappearing at the door
The "whomp" of his heavy body
Hitting the floor
As he jumps off the couch
His head near mine
On the pillow of the bed

The Blues

I picture the COVID virus
As an amorphous blue light
Illuminating a member of the family
Or a close friend in a small group

That person talks
The light emanates
From his mouth
Traveling as a blue fog
Into the air

She walks
The blue light follows
As a wedding train
Fluffy and flounced

Children can be blue
Despite their youthful vigor
I yearn to touch them.
I refrain

Night in the Pandemic

It is dark and quiet on the road
There have never been streetlights
But now no cars go by
In the houses only a few windows
are lit
I go through my bedtime routine
Turn down the heat
Switch off lights
As I head up the stairs
I look through the French doors
in the back of the house
And see the white full moon
Illuminating the dark silence

Long COVID

For three years
I have been masked, vaccinated
Intimidated from attending
Movies, restaurants,
Birthday parties, weddings
Fearing touching, hugging
Kissing.
Covid snuck in anyway
Stuck me in hospitals
With spiking fevers and cough
Pneumonia sapping my strength

Into the fourth year
Still testing and requesting
Others to test
Still avoiding crowds
No singing, drinking,
Eating together inside
I am shy
Of touching
Of hugging, of kissing
But I long for it all.

The Kiss

They leave their shoes at the door
His beat-up sneakers
Her low boots with the heel
She places the toes of her boots
Atop the toes of his sneakers

Paradise Lost

At age sixteen
He loses his best friend
To a car accident
Inexperienced driving
Alone
On a dark night

Now he has experience
With deep grief
Basketball in the afternoon
Death that night
He leaves school
When he hears the news

His other friends
Join him to visit their haunts
Gym, hockey rink, basketball court
They crowd into
The family's home
To share
Shock and sorrow

He is a pallbearer
Lifting his heavy load
Trying to absorb loss
To make meaning
From tragedy
To go on:
Changed

As Time Goes By

What is Missing:

Cartwheels in the dewy grass
Riding my bike to the pool
Ice skating on Opperman's Pond
Snow shoeing on the Rail Trail
Walking fearless on ice
Dancing with abandon
Sound of children's feet running upstairs
Easy companionship with a long-time partner

What Endures:

Small birds singing in the cold morning
Snow striping the north side of tree trunks
Red berries popping in white fields
A lighted Christmas tree on the porch
Sun warming the crocheted blanket over my legs
Tea steeping in the afternoon
Max the cat snuggling with me on the couch
Friends listening and laughing

Unburdened

To shake all cares and business
from our age
Conferring them on younger strengths,
while we
Unburdened, crawl toward death
> —King Lear

Unburdened by the body's frailty
Locked knees, loosened bowels
Weakened breath, watery eyes
By the brain's fog
Car keys in the freezer
Cell phone in the toilet

Unburdened by sleeplessness
By fears of the future
Hospital horrors
Nursing home nightmares
Losing friends and family
To death, despair

To be unburdened:
"There's the rub"
Before we crawl toward death.

Aging in Place

I build the little red house
in my early sixties
High toilets, wide doorways
A den downstairs across from
a full bath with walk-in shower
Two large bedrooms upstairs
Mine painted lavender
Guest room bright yellow.

It's been fifteen years
The stairs to the second floor
are steeper,
despite the extra railing
I love my lavender bedroom
Its large bed with fluffy down cover
Soft grey carpet.
Despite pleas from my children
I resist moving downstairs

Until Covid hits.
Hospitalization, weakness.
I paint the walls of the den
deep rose
Buy an adjustable single bed
Move the antique dresser and chair
The old-school clock on the wall
Ticks on

The Big D

My mother reacted to our moods
As children, by saying,
"You must be tired" or
"You are probably hungry."
Looking back, for the most part,
I now agree with her.
Naps are a rejuvenating pleasure
And tea and toast at four
Can calm my erratic heart.

My father, a sensitive soul,
Was finally diagnosed with what
Was then known as "manic-depression"
And now referred to as "bi-polar disorder."
His moods, the wild euphoria of the artist
Or the voice on the phone
That sounded as if he were talking underwater
Could not be cured with rest or food
But only treated with alcohol.

Now, so many years later,
Both parents long gone,
When I feel sad or angry,
Irritable or frustrated,
I take my naps and eat my toast
But if the world turns grey
And I cannot sleep or taste,
I fear the Big D.

Day and Night

During the week,
I swim at Mike Arteaga's Health Club
Walk on the Wallkill Valley Rail Trail
Knit a tweed hat for Mindy
Take a zoom yoga class

At night, I dream I cannot
find my locker at school.
All my books and papers
are in there.
No one can tell me where it is
or the combination to the lock.

The yoga teacher intones,
"Breathe in the color red
and release all fear.'

Last year, I install solar panels
on my roof
Purchase a new furnace
Rent my house for the summer
Publish a book of poetry

At night, I dream I am in
an unfamiliar country
I cannot remember the name
or location of my hotel.
Everyone is speaking a
foreign language.

Breathe in the color red
and release all fear.

I wake in the morning
to a sparkling winter day
I eat homemade granola,
drink fragrant hot coffee.
I speak to my children,
my friends
I revel in the joy and
ease of my life.

At night, I dream I am
driving my car
I cannot reach the brake,
and am heading down
a steep hill, with a
busy crossroad at
the stop sign.

Breathe in the color red,
and release all fear.

Battleground

It is becoming
a war on all fronts
Chronic auto-immune disease
of the joints
Muscle-wasting disease
Pre-cancerous skin lesions
Spinal stenosis, arthritis
Thinning bones
Underactive thyroid
Recurrent urinary tract infections
Kidney infections
Sepsis

The body sends out
its defensive troops
Doctors employ
their offensive arsenal:
High dose prednisone
HUMIRA injections
Antibiotics
Levothyroxine
Infusions for bone strength,
surgically remove
offensive enemies,
repair the ramparts

Moments of stasis
Resting in the
quiet bunker
until a new attack
lights up the foxhole,
scattering peace

Despite the
successful skirmishes,
it is increasingly clear
this war will not be won

Time Tempering

Babies' hair, gossamer stuff
Tufts of cotton
Matching silken skin
Before all is exposed to the earth
Its harsh winds, cold, heat
Time's tempering

My hair is now curly
In my youth and middle age
It was stick straight
Do the curls come with the grey?
Or maybe those heavy doses of prednisone
Are to blame

My hair was blond, then ash
Now gray and grayer
Soon it may be totally white
Is that me in the mirror?
Sometimes when I look quickly
I see my mother

Giving

My mother asks me
To clip her gnarled toenails
Before she is taken by ambulance
To the hospice where she dies

I don't think anything of it
At the time
Just another way I can help
Like the rides to the hospital

For tests and treatment
The beef stew I make
Which she says was delicious
But never ate

I give without thinking
She asks for so little
But it makes me so happy
I can help

Now I am ten years older
Than she was when she died
And forced to ask for help
Myself

How hard that is
To admit to need
To forego independence
To feel vulnerable to age

To welcome a bag of groceries
A spray of wildflowers
A pot of pea soup
A visit on the porch

To say yes to a helping hand
To lean on a strong body
To receive a needed embrace
From those who love me

Giving is better than receiving,
they say
But receiving is a gift
I am learning to give

I Remember When . . .

I could turn cartwheels in the dewy grass
Bits of green grass sticking to my bare feet

I could jump rope Double Dutch
My feet pounding the rhythm ahead of my brain

I could ride my bike to the municipal pool
Climb the ladder, jump off the diving board
And swim to the other end

I could perform the cheerleading routines
Jumping, bouncing, kicking
Throughout the game and into overtime

And now, so many years later
I remember I can still walk

My legs register every step
That I was unaware of in my youth

The cane is essential
The stair rail is necessary
But I remember
That I can still walk

Skype

Remember the days
When we said that a camera
On the phone
Would be the worst invention?

A caller in the morning
Witnessing wrinkled pajamas
Sleep-creased cheeks
Hair wildly askew

A caller at breakfast
Seeing egg on the face
Toast crumbs on a shirtfront
Messy counter in the background

A caller in the afternoon
Catching signs of a tear
Downturned mouth quivering
Unmade bed unbidden

The worst has come true
Even with preparation
Hair combed, chin up
Smile pasted on

I see what he sees
An old lady
Sagging neck, thinning hair
In the corner of the screen

Time and Again

My nod to Christmas
And light in the winter night
Is a small live tree
On my porch table
Draped with white lights
That come on each night
Casting hope both out to the road
And into my home

It is February
And still so cold
I cannot bear to disrobe
The still-fresh tree and drag it
Through icy ground
To its ignominious end
In the compost heap

Even though it keeps tipping over
In the winter winds
And I must drag
My now fragile body
Into the cold
To right it
Time and again

Settling

The clock ticks
The room is slightly cool
Redolent with the smell
of wood paneling
We sit in a silent circle
Breathing deeply
Muscles slowly relax

My monkey mind
Hops, jumps
Cackles and screeches
Bumping into the inner
shell of my skull
The body is quiet
The breath deepens

Finally, the monkey settles
He sits cross-legged
His hands open on his knees
His face slack and still
Eyes closed
He rests
From the relentlessness of activity
He settles

How Will I Know?

How will I know
When it is time to give up
My cozy red house
Light shining on yellow pine floors
Chickadees, cardinals at the bird feeder
Orange tulips on the dining table
Max the cat resting against my legs
Stretched on the couch

How will I know
When it is time to relinquish my car
And rely on the generosity
Of friends and family
All spontaneity squashed

How will I know
To be gracious
To cherish small joys
To welcome visitors
And new friends
To refrain from complaint
And recriminations
And not wish too hard for death

The End

The Indian Burial Ground
Is where I long ago decided
My ashes should rest
Drawn to the idea
That Indians would scalp
Their enemies to let out
Their departed souls
Through the tops of their heads

Now, so many years later
The Indian Burial Ground
Has succumbed to nature
A mass of impenetrable brambles
Do I want my children
To fight their way
Into an overgrown memory
To scatter my ashes?

The Oak Bluffs Cemetery plot
Next to my best friend Phyllis
Near the library and the Town Hall
Bucolic sweep of trees, flowers
Close to our summer cottages
No ticks, no prickles to avoid
Homecoming

About the Author

Susan Webber has been writing poetry since her teen years. She is a retired teacher who enjoys reading, yoga, meditation, swimming, knitting, and spending time with family and friends. She lives in New Paltz, New York.

www.ingramcontent.com/pod-product-compliance
Lightning Source LLC
Chambersburg PA
CBHW022145160426
43197CB00009B/1435